I AM THAT **WOMAN:**
WHO NEVER GAVE UP

Finding Strength and Success
in Adversity.

ELIZAGETH G. COLELLA

TABLE OF CONTENTS

INTRODUCTION

In a world often marred by challenges and uncertainties, there emerge remarkable souls who serve as beacons of unwavering strength and inspiration. These extraordinary individuals, much like the protagonist of our story, radiate a profound sense of humanity and resilience. This is the heartfelt chronicle of "That Woman Who Never Gave Up."

Life's journey can often resemble a stormy sea, filled with crests of joy and troughs of sorrow. Yet, within this narrative, you will discover someone whose unwavering spirit defied the darkest clouds and navigated through the fiercest of tempests. It's a story that speaks directly to the weary and the anxious heart.

As we begin this journey, you'll come to know an individual whose early years were marked by adversity and hardship. Her childhood was a canvas upon which life's difficulties were etched, challenges that might have overwhelmed many. Paradoxically, it was these very trials that forged her spirit into an enduring flame of hope.

Chapter by chapter, we will uncover pivotal moments of her life, where dreams and aspirations began to blossom, like flowers in the desert. These dreams became the guiding stars that illuminated her path through life's most turbulent waters.

The journey commences with a choice, a choice to never surrender, regardless of how daunting the path ahead may seem. In the chapters that follow, you will witness the struggles she faced, and her unwavering determination to overcome them. Her story is a soothing balm for those who feel weary and anxious, a testament to the strength that resides within.

But this narrative is not merely about hardship; it's also about triumph. For every setback, there were moments of celebration, bright stars that shone in the darkest of nights. It's a journey marked by resilience and a deep-rooted belief in the human spirit.

Within these pages, you'll also meet the individuals who served as pillars of support in her life – friends, family, mentors – all of whom offered solace and strength during trying times. Their presence highlights the importance of a loving support system in a world filled with challenges.

As you turn the pages, you will uncover invaluable lessons that will gently soothe the weary heart and ease the anxious mind. These are lessons about strength, about rising after every fall, about pursuing one's dreams, and, above all, about never giving up. This is a story that extends a warm embrace to all who have faced adversity.The chapters ahead will reveal a story of unwavering hope, boundless determination, and a love for life that shines through the darkest of days. It's a narrative that seeks to uplift and comfort, reminding each of us that, no matter the trials we face, there's a wellspring of strength within our hearts.

Join us on this journey as we explore the life and legacy of "That Woman Who Never Gave Up." Her story is not just a biography; it's a loving embrace for the weary and anxious hearts of the world, a source of comfort and inspiration.

Chapter 1: Early Struggles

In the tapestry of life, the early years of our protagonist were woven with threads of challenge and difficulty. Her childhood, much like a heart's first beat, was an intricate rhythm of struggle and survival that played out against a backdrop of uncertainty.

These were the formative years that etched indelible marks upon her young soul, and they stand as a testament to the strength that can bloom amidst adversity. Her story speaks directly to the hearts that have faced adversity, a gentle reminder that the most delicate flowers can push through the toughest soil.

During these days, the world may have seemed harsh and unrelenting, yet the young protagonist found the courage to take her first steps on this path called life.

She exemplified that the most fragile and tender beginnings can harbor the seeds of immense resilience.

The lessons of early hardship were not always easy, and the struggles were as harsh as winter winds. Yet, her life was a testament to the human spirit's innate capacity to find warmth and growth even in the coldest of winters.

Despite the hurdles, her spirit remained unwavering, like a lighthouse guiding ships through the darkest of nights. The early chapters of her life reveal a gentle resilience, a lesson for all weary hearts, that even in the face of adversity, the human spirit can weather the storm and emerge stronger.

These are the roots from which her story grew, and in every turn of the page, we will uncover the layers of determination, the whispered dreams that she held close to her heart, and the strength that lay hidden within her young soul.

As we venture deeper into this narrative, remember that her early struggles were not a tragedy but a symphony of resilience and hope. The compassion and strength she demonstrated in these formative years are a testament to the beauty that can emerge from the ashes of hardship.

In this chapter, we extend our empathy to the young heart that carried the weight of the world and found its rhythm in the face of adversity. These early struggles, though painful, are the foundation upon which the edifice of her life was built—a life that would inspire countless others to face their own trials with unwavering grace.

CHAPTER 2:

THE JOURNEY BEGINS

In the grand tapestry of life, the story of our protagonist continued to unfold, marked by an unshakeable resolve to face adversity head-on. This chapter delves into the pivotal moments when her journey truly began, and the lessons she learned from her early trials.

The young protagonist's journey was, in many ways, akin to setting sail on a vast, uncharted sea. The waves were unpredictable, and the winds sometimes fierce, but she hoisted her sails with a spirit undeterred by the unknown. These were the moments when her unwavering determination began to shape her destiny.

This chapter encapsulates a young woman who, with each step forward, faced challenges head-on. She regarded adversity not as an insurmountable wall but as a stepping stone, a platform from which to leap toward her aspirations. Her life was a testament to the fact that the journey is just as important, if not more so, than the destination.

In her pursuit of dreams and ambitions, she found allies and mentors who recognized her potential and offered guidance and support. It was during these early years that the seeds of inspiration were planted. Her mentors nurtured her dreams and instilled in her the belief that she could make them come true.

In the heart of this chapter lies the profound realization that her journey was not solitary. It was a collective effort, a testament to the strength of the human spirit, and the ability to inspire others with unwavering determination.
Her story, even at this early stage, was becoming a beacon of hope and an example of what could be achieved with persistence and a courageous heart.

As we venture deeper into this narrative, remember that life's journey often begins with a single step, and every challenge is an opportunity to learn and grow. In the chapters that follow, we will explore how this courageous spirit met with triumphs and setbacks, and how they ultimately led her down the path to success.

CHAPTER 3:

TRIUMPHS AND SETBACKS

Amidst the backdrop of life's unpredictable narrative, a unique tale unfolded in the quaint town of Riverbrook. Our protagonist, Lily, was a young woman whose journey mirrored the ebbs and flows of the town's serene river. In Riverbrook, where dreams whispered in the wind and aspirations bloomed like wildflowers along the riverbanks, Lily's story began.

Lily's dream was simple yet profound: she aspired to become an accomplished artist. Her brushstrokes were imbued with a vitality that breathed life into her canvas, and the world began to notice her remarkable talent. Her first triumph came when she was selected to showcase her paintings at the town's annual art exhibition.

The exhibition was a moment of celebration for Riverbrook, and Lily's achievement was a source of pride for the entire town.

Her paintings, vibrant and evocative, became a bridge between her heart and those who beheld her art. It was a triumph that resonated with her unwavering dedication.

However, in the midst of her growing success, an unexpected setback loomed like a tempest on the horizon. Just days before the exhibition, a severe storm surged through Riverbrook, causing extensive damage, including to the venue. The exhibition was in jeopardy, and the setback weighed heavily on Lily's heart.

It was a test of her resilience, a challenge to her unwavering determination. Instead of surrendering to despair, Lily rallied the town's artists and residents. They worked tirelessly, transforming the battered venue into a testament of collective strength. It became a symbol of Riverbrook's resilience and Lily's unwavering spirit.

When the exhibition finally opened its doors, it was not just a showcase of art but a testament to the town's ability to endure and emerge stronger in the face of adversity. Lily's triumph was not just a personal achievement; it embodied the spirit of triumph over setbacks that defined Riverbrook.

This chapter is a reflection of the interplay between triumphs and setbacks in Lily's life and the town of Riverbrook. It serves as a reminder that, even when facing the harshest storms, resilience and determination can lead to the most Beautiful triumphs, not only for oneself but for an entire community.

Chapter 4: LESSONS AND LEGACY

In the intricate narrative of Lily's life, Chapter 4 is a poignant exploration of the lessons she learned along her remarkable journey and the legacy she began to craft for generations to come.

As her story continued to unfold, the significance of every challenge and every triumph became clear. Each hurdle she had faced was a teacher, imparting valuable insights about resilience, perseverance, and the enduring strength of the human spirit.

Lily recognized that success was not merely a destination but a journey in itself. Her pursuit of dreams was not just about achieving goals but about embracing the process with grace and courage. This was a lesson she carried with her, a reminder that the path to success was paved with both triumphs and setbacks.

The significance of her mentors, those who had guided her with wisdom and kindness, was not lost on her. Their legacy, intertwined with hers, served as a source of inspiration for her as she, in turn, became a mentor to budding artists. It was her way of nurturing the seeds of inspiration in the hearts of others, just as her mentors had done for her.

But the most profound lesson of all was the understanding that her journey was not solitary. It was a shared endeavor, a testament to the strength of the human spirit.
 The legacy she was crafting was not just about personal achievements but about

illuminating the path for others, reminding them that resilience and determination could transform dreams into reality.

In the chapters that follow, we will explore how Lily's life story continued to evolve, how her lessons and legacy expanded, and how the indomitable spirit she embodied resonated through the generations that followed. This chapter serves as a poignant reminder that even the most intricate tapestry of life is woven from simple yet powerful threads of wisdom, perseverance, and inspiration.

Chapter 5: INSPIRING RESILIENCE

Lily's legacy, born from her lessons and experiences, continued to thrive. The town of Riverbrook had transformed into an artistic hub, where the spirit of creativity thrived in the heart of every resident. The legacy of her art workshops had become a cornerstone of the community.

In her twilight years, Lily took on the role of a mentor, not just to artists but to all who sought inspiration. She shared the wisdom she had gathered, the lessons she had learned, and the strength she had acquired throughout her life's journey. Her home became a haven for those in need of encouragement and guidance.

As she continued to nurture the dreams of young artists, she encountered an extraordinary tale of resilience in a young woman named Emily. Emily had faced her fair share of challenges and setbacks but possessed a spirit that refused to yield to adversity. Lily saw herself in Emily, a reflection of the young artist she once was.

Here is a Little story

In the tranquil heart of Riverbrook, where art and aspiration danced like whispers on the wind, Lily embarked on a journey of mentorship. Her home became a sanctuary for budding artists, a haven where dreams took shape on canvases and in the hearts of those who dared to dream.

One bright morning, a young woman named Emily walked into Lily's life. Emily's spirit was an unyielding force, like the river's steady flow that would not be dammed by adversity. Her journey was etched with trials and tribulations, but her spirit remained unbroken. In Emily, Lily saw a reflection of her own youth, the days when her canvas was blank, and her dreams vast and uncharted.

Lily recognized the spark in Emily's eyes, a spark she knew all too well, the spark of an artist driven by the undying desire to create. They began to paint side by side, not just on canvases but in their shared experiences. Lily became not just a mentor but a confidante, offering not only artistic guidance but life's wisdom.

Over cups of tea and shared laughter, Emily's story unfolded. She had faced adversity that would have left many defeated. Illness had whispered in her ear, challenging her very will to paint, but she refused to be silenced. The setback became a stepping stone, and her spirit soared with resilience.

In Emily's unwavering determination, Lily saw a reflection of herself, the young artist who had confronted the world with a canvas and a dream. She shared stories of her own triumphs and setbacks, weaving a tapestry of inspiration for the young artist who, against all odds, dared to believe in herself.

Together, they painted not just strokes of art but strokes of courage. Emily's art flourished, her spirit found new heights, and her smile became a beacon of hope. She was not just a student; she was a cherished friend, a testament to the enduring strength of the human spirit.

In the heart of Riverbrook, the town's canvas was transformed. It was no longer just a place of art but a place where resilience and inspiration flowed like a river, reflecting the remarkable journey of two artists—Lily, the mentor, and Emily, the mentee.

Lily took Emily under her wing, offering not just artistic guidance but life lessons as well. She shared stories of her own triumphs and setbacks, imparting the invaluable understanding that every obstacle could be surmounted with unwavering determination.

The bond between Lily and Emily grew stronger with each passing day. Emily's art blossomed, and her spirit found new strength. She became not just a student but a cherished friend, and together, they painted the town of Riverbrook with the colors of resilience and inspiration.

In the heart of this chapter lies the essence of Lily's life journey: a reminder that even as we age, our capacity to inspire and uplift others remains undiminished. Her legacy was not just a tale of her accomplishments but a living testament to the enduring strength of the human spirit.

As Lily's story reaches its conclusion, we celebrate not just the artist she became but the mentor, the friend, and the beacon of hope that she embodied. Her legacy was a reminder that life's most profound impact isn't measured in personal achievements but in the

resilience and inspiration we pass on to
others.

CHAPTER 6: THE COLORS OF CHANGE

In the heart of Riverbrook, where the rhythm of life swayed with the seasons, Lily's haven of art thrived. The town had witnessed transformations, not only in its landscapes but also in the lives of its inhabitants. The colors of change painted a mesmerizing tableau, and it was a chapter in Lily's life where her mentorship would take an unexpected turn.

One crisp autumn morning, as the leaves danced on the wind's melody, a man named Daniel wandered into Lily's art sanctuary. He was a fisherman, grizzled by years spent navigating the tempestuous seas, and a stranger to the world of art. His hands had become calloused from the harsh ropes and salty waters, not from wielding a brush.

For Daniel, the sea had been both a source of sustenance and a canvas of treacherous challenges. His life had been etched in the tempestuous hues of the ocean, its ever-shifting shades reflecting his journey of highs and lows. The relentless waves, at times turbulent and formidable, had been both his adversary and his companion.

Lily, with her warm smile, welcomed this unlikely candidate into her world of colors and canvas. She handed him a blank sheet, and he hesitated for a moment, the paper a stark contrast to the endless expanse of the sea. But as he dipped his brush into the palette, something extraordinary happened.

With each stroke, Daniel found solace in the gentle cadence of art. The colors he applied were like echoes of the sea, from the deep blues of stormy nights to the serene turquoise of tranquil mornings. His work was not just art; it was a reflection of his life, of the ocean that had shaped him. As he painted, the lines etched on his face seemed to soften, and a sense of tranquility washed over him.

The transformation was not just evident in his art, but also in his perspective on life. He began to see the sea not only as an adversary but as a wellspring of inspiration. The challenges he had faced at sea, once seen as obstacles, became opportunities to depict the resilience of the human spirit.

In his newfound passion for art, he discovered a bridge between the world he had known and the world he had yet to explore. The turbulent sea was now mirrored in his paintings, and he found in art a way to communicate emotions he had never put into words.

Daniel's metamorphosis became a testament to the power of change, a reminder that life's hues were as diverse as a painter's palette. The artist within him had emerged, and it was a transformation that enriched not only his own life but also the canvas of Riverbrook's community.

As the sun dipped below the horizon, painting the sky with shades of orange and purple, Daniel stepped back from his canvas, a sense of fulfillment in his heart. He gazed at his painting, seeing not just the strokes of paint but the journey he had embarked upon.

In this chapter, Riverbrook saw not only the change of seasons but the transformation of a man who had found solace and beauty in the unexpected world of art. It was a chapter that painted a vivid picture of the universality of art's healing touch, how it could infuse life with colors of change and transformation, even in the most unexpected of souls.

CHAPTER 7: ECHOES OF INSPIRATION

In Riverbrook, the legacy of Lily's artistry continued to flourish, and like ripples in a tranquil pond, it extended its reach beyond the town's borders. An art exhibition, curated by Lily, beckoned artists from far and wide. The town's modest gallery had transformed into a treasure trove of creativity, a place where colors and forms painted stories, and art whispered secrets.

Among the attendees was Maria, a gifted sculptor from a neighboring town. Her sculptures breathed with a lifelike grace, each piece capturing the essence of the human spirit. Yet, despite her talent, Maria often felt a certain solitude in her artistic journey. Her creations were masterful, but she longed for something more, something that transcended the confines of her studio.

The moment Maria stepped into the gallery, her eyes fell upon Lily's paintings. They spoke of a life well-lived, of dreams pursued, and of the enduring spirit of art. An invisible thread of connection wove through the air, binding Maria to the gallery and its curator, Lily.

Lily, perceptive as ever, noticed Maria's fascination with her work. They began to converse, their words flowing like a duet of voices, one speaking the language of paint, the other the language of form. Lily expressed her admiration for the life Maria's sculptures breathed into clay, and Maria shared her fascination with the colors and brushstrokes that danced on Lily's canvases.

As their worlds intertwined, a unique connection formed. Lily's foray into the world of three-dimensional art began, guided by Maria's expert hands. Clay and bronze became her new canvas, and together, they sculpted pieces that transcended the boundaries of artistic expression.

Maria, in turn, learned from Lily that the power of connection could breathe new life into her creations. Her sculptures, once solitary, began to find new depth and meaning. They weren't just representations of forms but reflections of the interplay between art and the human experience.

It was a chapter that celebrated the endless wellspring of inspiration that art could offer, transcending the confines of mediums and forging connections that transcended boundaries. As Lily's legacy rippled further, her gallery became a haven for artists of all kinds. The whispers of artistic secrets and the echoes of inspiration became a song that resonated not just within the gallery's walls but in the hearts of those who passed through them.

The gallery, once a modest space, now embodied the spirit of Riverbrook, a testament to the power of art to forge connections and breathe new life into the creations of those who dared to dream. As artists from far and wide left the gallery, they carried with them not just memories of beautiful art but the imprints of profound connections, connections that transcended the boundaries of canvas and sculpture.

CHAPTER 8: THE PORTRAIT OF HOPE

Time, like a river, flows steadily through Riverbrook, and Lily's age becomes more apparent in her stride. The town watched as the seasons turned, each year adding another layer of wisdom to her soul. Her health had become fragile, and she faced her own share of setbacks, but the seeds of hope she had sown in the hearts of the community began to flourish in ways she could never have foreseen.

As the years passed, Lily became a revered figure in Riverbrook, not just as an artist but as a symbol of resilience and inspiration. The young artists she had mentored, those who had once come to her with eager hearts and blank canvases, had now grown into accomplished individuals, thanks to her guidance and unwavering support.

One bright spring day, a group of these young artists gathered in the heart of Riverbrook.

They had a plan, one that would pay tribute to the mentor who had shaped their artistic journeys and, in doing so, had shaped their lives. Their goal was to create a mural, a masterpiece that would honor Lily's life and the lives she had touched.

The mural, larger than life, would depict scenes from Lily's journey, from the early days when she had courageously wielded her first brush to her days as a mentor, sharing her wisdom and nurturing the dreams of others. It was a monumental task, but the spirit of community and the inspiration she had imparted fueled their passion.

They worked day and night, with each brushstroke and each color infused with the memories of their shared experiences with Lily. The mural became a collective effort, an expression of the impact she had on all their lives. It was not just art; it was a testament to the beauty of resilience, a reminder that life's setbacks could be transformed into hope and inspiration.

The day the mural was unveiled was a moment of pure magic. Residents of Riverbrook gathered in front of the mural, their eyes filled with awe and their hearts with gratitude. They saw not just strokes of paint but the legacy of a woman who had dedicated her life to art and to inspiring others.

The mural stood as a symbol of hope, an emblem of the strength of the human spirit, and a reminder that art could be a testament to the beauty of resilience. It whispered to all who gazed upon it that every setback could be transformed into a masterpiece, that every challenge could become a source of inspiration, and that the colors of hope could shine even in the face of adversity.

Lily watched with tears in her eyes, her heart swelling with pride for the young artists who had not only paid tribute to her but had given the town a beacon of hope. In that moment, she realized that the true measure of a life well-lived was not in the accolades received but in the lives touched and the inspiration kindled in the hearts of others.

As she looked upon the mural, she knew that her legacy was not only in the strokes of her brush but in the echoes of hope that now resided within the hearts of the community. The mural became a living testament, and Lily found hope not just in her own heart but in the eyes and smiles of all who passed by it, a reminder that art was a canvas on which resilience and inspiration could flourish in the most beautiful of ways.

CHAPTER 9: THE ART OF GIVING BACK

As the tapestry of Lily's life unfolded with the passage of time, her legacy continued to evolve. In her later years, she recognized the profound impact that art had on her own journey and the lives of those she had touched. With a heart full of gratitude and an unwavering desire to give back, she embarked on a new chapter.

In the heart of Riverbrook, she established the "Lily Art Foundation." This foundation, like a nurturing mother to burgeoning artists, aimed to support the talented but underprivileged individuals whose dreams were as vivid as the colors on Lily's canvases.
The foundation became a beacon of hope, a testament to the importance of giving

back to the community that had nurtured her own artistic spirit.

It was a chapter that underscored the belief that the true measure of one's journey lay in how it enriched the lives of others.

The foundation's impact was profound. It provided scholarships to aspiring artists, ensuring that financial constraints would not stifle their creative passions. It furnished art supplies to those who had the talent but lacked the means to express it. It offered mentorship, drawing from the rich reservoir of artists and mentors that Lily had met throughout her own journey.

` In the heart of Riverbrook, the foundation's influence was like a brush dipped in vibrant hues, painting the town with opportunities, inspiration, and possibilities. Young artists found in it not just support but also a profound belief in their potential. The flame of inspiration, kindled by Lily, now blazed even brighter, lighting the paths of many.

Through the years, the foundation's impact extended beyond Riverbrook. It nurtured talents from neighboring towns, extending its hand of support to those who dared to dream and create. It was a reminder that the beauty of art could flourish, not just on canvas but in the lives of countless individuals.

Lily, in her twilight years, found solace and fulfillment in the knowledge that her legacy was not just about her own artistic accomplishments but in the lives she had touched and the dreams she had ignited. The art of giving back had enriched not only the community but had sown the seeds of inspiration for future generations.

In the heart of Riverbrook and beyond, the Lily Art Foundation was a testament to the idea that the true measure of one's journey was the difference one could make in the lives of others. It was a testament to the enduring power of art to inspire, uplift, and give back to a world that had given so much.

Chapter 10: The Masterpiece of a Life - Expanded Narrative

In the twilight of her life, Lily found herself in the familiar embrace of her art studio. The room was a sanctuary, filled with the countless canvases that told the story of her journey. The colors on the walls were like memories, each stroke a reflection of her determination, resilience, and the indomitable power of inspiration.

As she sat amidst the colors and canvases, the room seemed to come alive with the echoes of her journey. Each painting held a piece of her heart, a fragment of her experiences, and a whisper of the stories she had lived and inspired.

The journey had been, in every sense, a masterpiece. The canvas of her life had been painted with hues that ranged from the deep blues of early struggles to the vibrant yellows of accomplishments. It was a testament to the power of determination and the ability of the human spirit to rise above adversity.

Lily had not just been an artist; she had been a mentor, a friend, and a beacon of hope for the town of Riverbrook. Her legacy was not confined to the walls of her studio but was etched in the hearts of the community she had touched.

As she gazed at her life's work, she understood that the true measure of her journey was not in the strokes of her brush but in the lives she had influenced.

The young artists she had mentored had gone on to inspire others, creating a ripple effect of inspiration that transcended generations.

Her legacy was a living testament to the strength of the human spirit and the enduring power of art. The colors on her canvases were not just pigments on paper but reflections of the resilience that resided within her and within the hearts of all who had known her.

As she reflected on her journey, she knew that her story was not confined to the pages of a book or the walls of her studio. It was a timeless painting, a masterpiece that would continue to inspire the world for generations to come. It was a reminder that the impact of a life well-lived was not just in the moments experienced but in the enduring influence it left on the canvas of time.

CONCLUSION: A LIFE'S CANVAS

In the quiet town of Riverbrook, nestled between rolling hills and a winding river, the story of Lily unfolded like a vivid canvas. Hers was a journey that defied the constraints of age and transcended the boundaries of art. It was a life painted with the colors of determination, resilience, and unyielding inspiration.

Lily's legacy, like a river's gentle flow, had touched the lives of many. It had painted new dreams on the canvases of the young artists she had mentored. It had sculpted connections that transcended the confines of mediums and geographical boundaries. It had breathed life into the creations of those who dared to dream. It had been a testament to the beauty of resilience and a beacon of hope that shone through even the darkest of times.

As the pages of this book draw to a close, we are reminded that the impact of a life well-lived is not confined to the self but extends to the lives it touches. Lily's legacy, a tapestry of colors and stories, will continue to inspire the world for generations to come.

The canvas of her life, filled with strokes of passion and purpose, tells a story of the human spirit's ability to rise above adversity, to nurture dreams, and to give back to the world. Her journey teaches us that art, in all its forms, is a language of the heart, a language that can speak to the soul, heal wounds, and inspire resilience.

As we turn the final page of this book, we carry with us not just the story of Lily but the message that, like her, we too can paint our lives with the colors of determination, resilience, and inspiration. We can mentor, inspire, and give back, leaving our own indelible mark on the canvas of time.

Lily's story is a testament to the enduring power of art and the strength of the human spirit. It is a reminder that, in every stroke of the brush, in every sculpture formed, and in every connection forged, we have the capacity to inspire, to uplift, and to create a masterpiece of our own lives.

In the heart of Riverbrook, the legacy of Lily lives on, a symbol of the endless possibilities that await those who dare to dream and create. As we bid farewell to these pages, may we carry with us the colors of Lily's life and continue to paint our own stories with resilience, hope, and unwavering inspiration.

WRITE YOUR INSPIRATIONS HERE:

_____

_____
_____
_____
_____
_____
_____
_____
_____
_____
_____
_____
_____

www.ingramcontent.com/pod-product-compliance
Lightning Source LLC
Chambersburg PA
CBHW050521290526
45786CB00007B/2641